The KnowHow Book of Action Toys

Usborne Publishing

Written and devised by:
Heather Amery

Contributors: Christopher Carey,
Andras Ranki, Diane Dorgan,
Leonard Smith, Andrew Calder

Designed by:
David Armitage and Patricia Lee
Illustrated by:
Neil Ross

Educational Adviser:
Frank Blackwell

First published in 1975
Usborne Publishing Ltd
20 Garrick Street
London WC2E 9BJ

Printed in Great Britain by
W S Cowell Ltd
Ipswich

About this Book

This is a book about lots of
toys, machines, models and
games to make and work. For
most of them, all you need are
paper, cardboard, plastic
bottles and cartons, cardboard
boxes and tubes, straws and
plasticine. You can probably
find most of these at home.
The measurements we have
given are only a guide. You
can make the things any size
you like.

When you make the toys and
machines, you can cover them
with coloured paper as you go
along, or paint them when they
are finished.

Remember to use quick-drying
strong glue, such as Bostik I or
UHU, except for sticking
expanded polystyrene tiles.
For this you need a glue used
for sticking material, such as
Copydex.

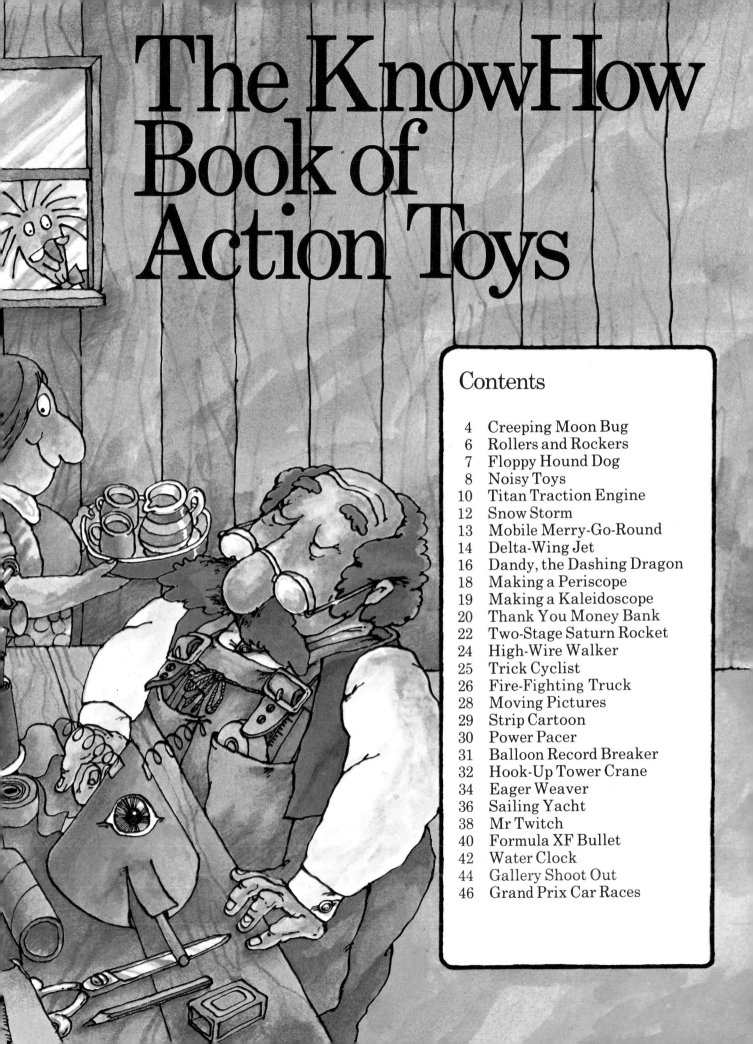

The KnowHow Book of Action Toys

Contents

4   Creeping Moon Bug
6   Rollers and Rockers
7   Floppy Hound Dog
8   Noisy Toys
10 Titan Traction Engine
12 Snow Storm
13 Mobile Merry-Go-Round
14 Delta-Wing Jet
16 Dandy, the Dashing Dragon
18 Making a Periscope
19 Making a Kaleidoscope
20 Thank You Money Bank
22 Two-Stage Saturn Rocket
24 High-Wire Walker
25 Trick Cyclist
26 Fire-Fighting Truck
28 Moving Pictures
29 Strip Cartoon
30 Power Pacer
31 Balloon Record Breaker
32 Hook-Up Tower Crane
34 Eager Weaver
36 Sailing Yacht
38 Mr Twitch
40 Formula XF Bullet
42 Water Clock
44 Gallery Shoot Out
46 Grand Prix Car Races

Creeping Moon Bug

Wind up the motor on this Moon Bug. Put the Bug down and watch it creep along very slowly.

You will need
an empty cotton reel
a used matchstick
a strong rubber band
a candle
a stick, about 10 cm long
a sheet of thick paper
thick cardboard
corrugated cardboard
thin, bendy wire
a table knife
a pencil and scissors

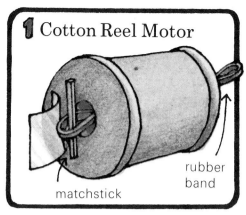

1 Cotton Reel Motor

matchstick • rubber band

Push the rubber band through the cotton reel. Push a short bit of matchstick through the loop at one end. Stick the matchstick down with a bit of tape.

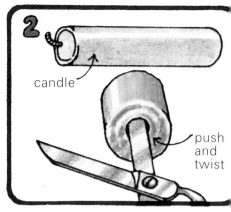

candle • push and twist

Slice a ring, about 1 cm wide, off the end of a candle with a table knife. Make a hole through it with one blade of the scissors.

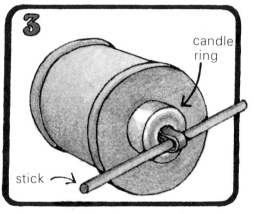

candle ring • stick

Push the free end of the rubber band through the candle ring. Then put the stick through the loop.

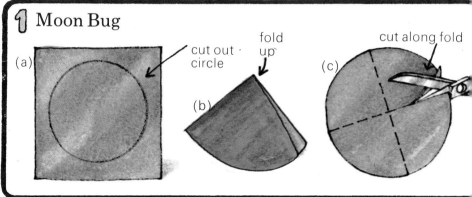

1 Moon Bug

(a) cut out circle • fold up (b) • cut along fold (c)

Draw a circle on thick paper (a). Cut it out. Fold the circle in half and then in half again (b). Unfold the paper and cut along one crease to the middle (c).

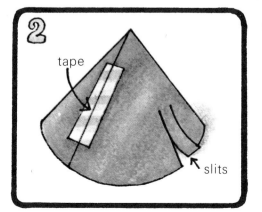

tape • slits

Curl the paper round to make a cone. Stick the edges together with tape. Cut two slits in the cone to make a flap.

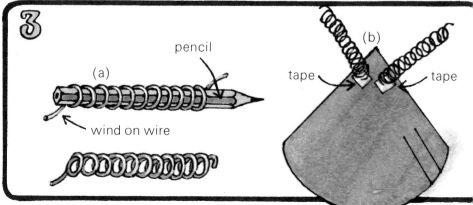

(a) pencil • wind on wire • (b) tape • tape

To make the antennae, wind a piece of bendy wire round a pencil (a). Slide it off. Curl up a second piece and stick them on the paper cone with tape (b).

Wind up the cotton reel motor. Put the cone of the Moon Bug over it, with one end of the stick poking out through the flap.

1 Climbing Bug

draw round

cardboard

Put a cotton reel down on a piece of thick cardboard. Draw round it. Draw a second circle.

2

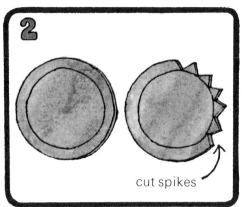

cut spikes

Cut out the two circles a bit bigger than the drawn lines. Cut out little bits all round both circles, like this.

3

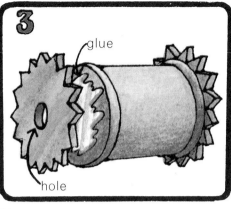

glue

hole

Glue a circle to each end of the cotton reel. Leave it to dry before making it into a Moon Bug.

4

Cut a long strip of corrugated cardboard about 5 cm wide. Make it into a steep road by putting things under it. Put the Bug at the bottom and let it climb.

Winding Up

wind round

Wind up the cotton reel by turning the stick round and round lots of times. Put the reel down. Put the cone over it with one end of the stick poking through the flap.

Rollers and Rockers

Jumping Bean

Make this Jumping Bean and stand it at the top of a gentle slope. Let it go and watch it jump and roll.

You will need
a ping pong ball
a piece of thick paper, about
   10 cm long and 5 cm wide
a marble
scissors
sticky tape

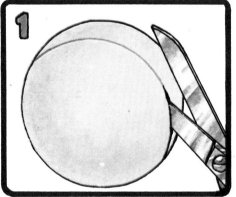

1 Push one blade of the scissors into the ping pong ball on the join line. Cut all the way round on the line.

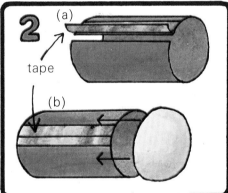

2 Roll the paper into a tube to fit just inside one half of the ping pong ball. Stick the tube with tape (a). Stick the tube to one half of the ball with tape (b).

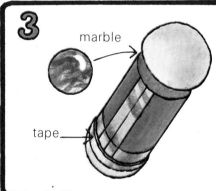

3 Put the marble in the tube. Stick the other half of the ball on the end of the tube with tape.

Rocking Egghead

Knock and push this Egghead in any way you like but he will always stand upright again.

You will need
a clean, dry eggshell with the
   top taken off
a lump of plasticine
a sheet of paper
a pencil
glue
paints
scissors

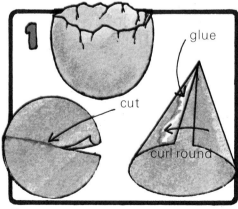

1 Draw a circle on a piece of paper, using a saucer as a guide. Cut out the circle and fold it in half. Cut along the fold. Roll one half into a cone and glue the edges.

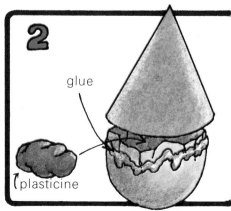

2 Stick a lump of plasticine in the bottom of the eggshell. Glue the cone to the top of the shell. Paint a funny face on it.

Floppy Hound Dog

Push the rubber bands hard to make the Dog flop about.

You will need
strong plastic carton
strong rubber bands
piece of kitchen foil rolled into a small ball
drinking straw
pieces of very strong thread, each about 20 cm long
big needle
piece of thin cardboard, about 4 cm long and 4 cm wide
small buttons
sticky tape and scissors

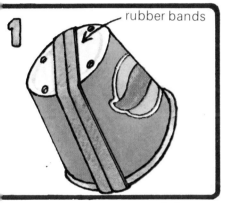

1 Put two rubber bands round the plastic carton. Poke four holes in the bottom of the carton, near the edges, with a needle.

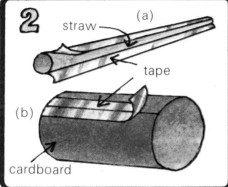

2 Roll the straw tightly in sticky tape (a). Cut it into 12 pieces, all the same length. Roll up the piece of cardboard into a tube. Stick it with tape (b).

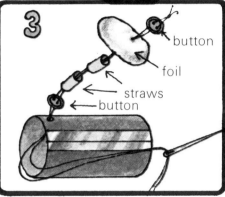

3 Knot two threads together. Thread the ends through a small button, the foil ball, two straw bits, another small button, and then the cardboard tube, like this.

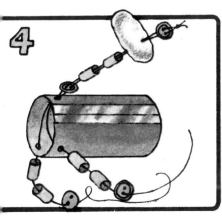

4 Pull one thread out of the needle hole. Push the other one through the other side of the tube, two straws and a button. Do the same with the other thread.

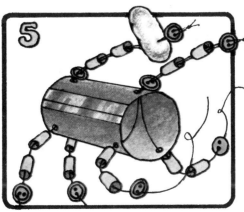

5 With two more threads, do the same at the other end of the tube to make the tail and the back legs, like this.

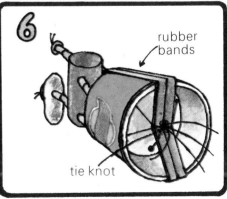

6 Push a thread through each hole in the bottom of the carton. Pull two threads down on each side of the rubber bands. Tie all the threads together very tightly.

Noisy Toys

Twirling Tweeter

Hold the end of the string and twirl the Tweeter round and round your head.

You will need

a very small plastic pot or tube
    with a lid
a piece of string, about 1 metre
    long
a used matchstick
sticky tape and scissors

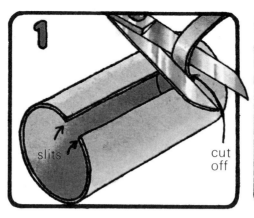

Take the lid off the plastic pot or tube. Cut two slits down one side, about $\frac{1}{2}$ cm apart. Bend back the flap and cut it off.

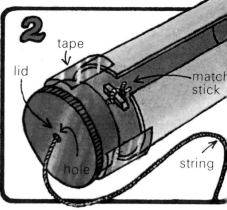

Make a hole in the lid. Push one end of a piece of string through and tie it round a matchstick. Put the lid on the pot and stick it down with tape.

Wailing Whirler

Hold the stick and swing the Whirler round and round it. Make sure the string is on the rosin. The faster the Whirler goes, the louder it will wail.

You will need

a thin stick or a pencil
a piece of nylon string or
    fishing line, about 30 cm long
a lump of rosin
    (this is sold in music shops)
a plastic carton or yoghurt pot
a used matchstick
glue and scissors

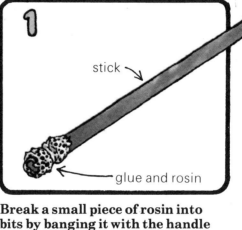

Break a small piece of rosin into bits by banging it with the handle of the scissors. Put glue on one end of the stick and dip it in the bits of rosin. Leave to dry.

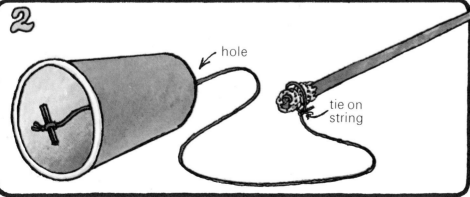

Make a hole in the bottom of a plastic carton. Push one end of the string through and tie a matchstick to the end, like this.

Loop the other end of the string loosely round the rosin on the end of the stick. Tie a knot.

Hanger Clanger

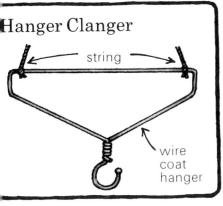

string

wire coat hanger

Tie the two pieces of string to a wire coat hanger, like this. Hold the other ends of the string in your ears. Bang the hanger against something and listen.

Roaring Ruler

Thread a piece of string through the hole in the end of a ruler or a thin, flat piece of wood. Tie a knot. Spin the ruler round your head to make a roaring noise.

Singing Bottle

cork

rub

Dip a cork in water and rub it on the side of a glass bottle. Try rubbing it gently and then hard to make bird singing noises.

Clucking Hen

Hold the carton in one hand. Hold the string very tightly between your fingers and thumb of the other hand and jerk them down the string.

You will need
2 plastic cartons or yoghurt pots
a piece of string, about 20 cm long
a used matchstick
a lump of rosin
quick-drying glue
scissors

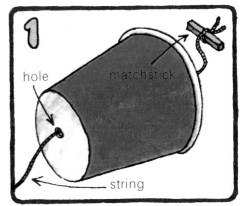

1

hole

matchstick

string

Make a hole in the bottom of a plastic carton. Push a piece of nylon thread through the hole. Tie it round a matchstick.

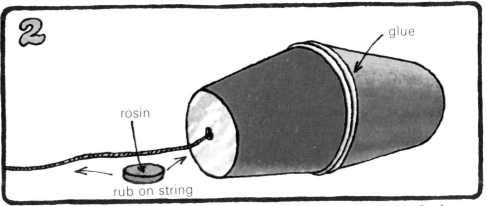

2

rosin

glue

rub on string

Glue a second carton to the first one, like this. Rub the string up and down on a piece of rosin.

When you have used the clucker a few times, rub on more rosin. Try making cluckers with smaller or larger plastic cartons to make different clucking noises.

Titan Traction Engine

You will need

a strong cardboard box, about 27
   cm long, 9 cm wide, 9 cm deep
thick cardboard
corrugated cardboard
2 small boxes, each about 12 cm
   long and 4 cm wide
a small, open cardboard box
5 cotton reels and 3 pencils
a cardboard tube, about 10 cm
   long
6 thin sticks or garden canes
a small polystyrene tray
1 egg holder cut from an egg box
sandpaper
scissors, glue, sticky tape,
   string, a saucer, a yoghurt pot

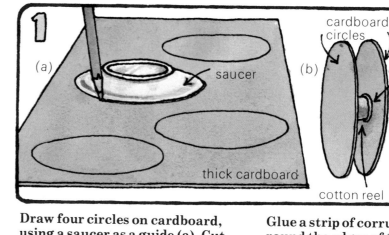

Draw four circles on cardboard,
using a saucer as a guide (a). Cut
them out. Glue one circle to each
end of a cotton reel (b). Glue the
other two circles to a second reel.

Glue a strip of corrugated cardboard
round the edges of two of the
cardboard circles, like this (c).
Do the same to the other two
cardboard circles.

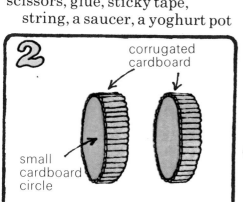

Make the front wheels in the same
way as the back ones, but much
smaller. The cardboard circles
should be about the same size as
the top of a small yoghurt pot.

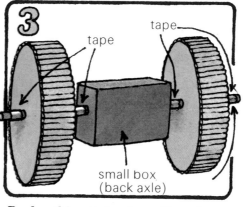

Push a thin stick, about 28 cm long,
through the middle of a small box.
Push one back wheel on to each end
of the stick. Wrap sticky tape round
the stick each side of both wheels.

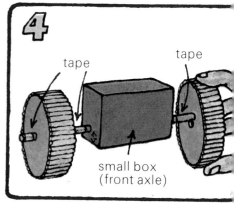

Push another stick through another
small box, about 1 cm from the base.
Push one front wheel on to each end
of the stick. Wrap sticky tape round
the stick each side of the wheels.

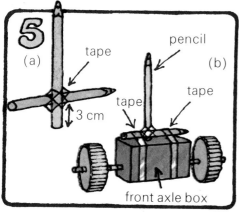

Tape two pencils together (a). Push
the upright pencil into the front
axle box, like this. Tape the other
pencil firmly to the axle box (b).

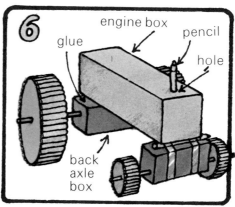

Glue the back axle box underneath
one end of a strong cardboard box.
Push the upright pencil on the
front axle box through a hole at
the other end of the box.

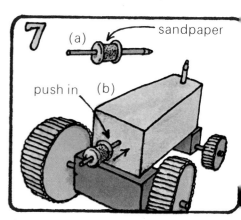

Glue corrugated cardboard or
sandpaper round the middle of a
cotton reel. Push a pencil through
the reel (a). Push the pencil point
into the back of the engine box (b).

Push this traction engine along and steer it by turning the cotton reel wheel.

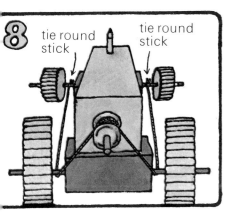

8

tie round stick   tie round stick

Wrap a piece of string round the reel, like this. Tie one end to one side of the front axle. Pull the other end tightly and tie it to the other side of the axle.

9

thin sticks

tape

Glue the open box to the back axle box, like this. Tape two sticks, about 26 cm long, to two corners. Push two sticks, about 15 cm long, into the engine box, as shown.

10

tray   egg holder

tube

glue

Put a polystyrene tray on top of the four sticks, like this. Glue a cardboard tube over the pencil at the front of the engine box. Put the egg holder on top of it.

Snow Storm

Make a mountain with little houses, or a hill, and stick on little plastic animals and people. Shake the jar to start the snow storm and watch it slowly settle.

You will need
a short glass jar with a
   screw-on lid
different coloured plasticine
waterproof inks
waterproof glue
french chalk (this is sold in
   chemist shops)
cold, boiled water

1 press in plasticine

glue

Take the lid off the jar. Spread glue on the inside. Press some plasticine on the glue, keeping it away from the edge of the lid.

2

Press on more plasticine to make a high mountain. Shape small blocks for houses. Draw in doors and windows with waterproof ink. Press them to the mountain.

3 french chalk

cold boiled water

Pour cold, boiled water into the jar, almost to the top. Put in one heaped teaspoon of french chalk. Stir it until all the lumps have been mixed in.

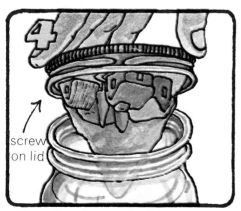

4

screw on lid

When the glue on the lid is dry, turn the lid over. Screw it on to the jar very tightly. Some of the water may run over.

Try making different scenes in other glass jars with lots of coloured plasticine.

You could make a Christmas scene and put gold and silver glitter bits in the water.

Mobile Merry-Go-Round

...nd up this mobile and hang it
...It will spin slowly round for
...te a long time.

...u will need
...lastic squeezy bottle
...ubber bands
...airpin
...n cardboard
...rinking straws
...eces of cotton thread, each
...bout 20 cm long
...encil and string
...ssors, glue and sticky tape

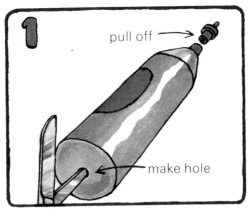

Pull off the top of the plastic bottle.
Make a hole in the bottom
with one blade of the scissors.

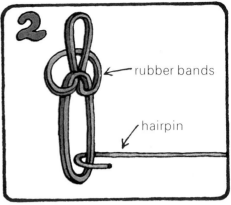

Loop two rubber bands together,
like this. Straighten a hairpin.
Bend one end into a hook and loop
it on to one rubber band.

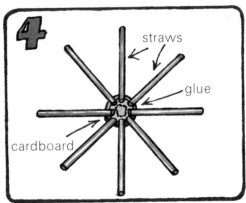

...rop the hairpin through the hole
...the plastic bottle. Put a pencil
...rough the end of the band. Push
...e hairpin through the bottle top
...d bend it over.

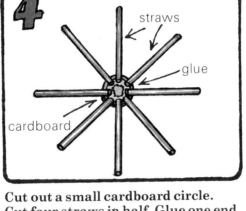

Cut out a small cardboard circle.
Cut four straws in half. Glue one end
of each straw to the circle, like this.

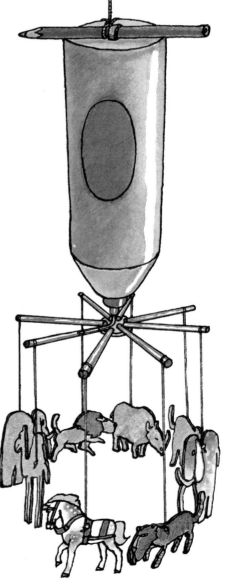

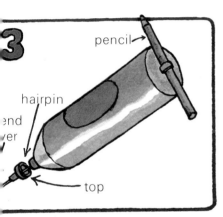

...raw eight small animals on thin
...ardboard. Cut them out. Glue one
...nd of each thread to an animal (a).
...lue the other end to a straw (b).

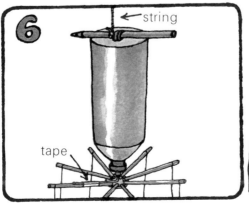

Stick the hairpin on the plastic
bottle to one straw, like this. Tie a
piece of string to the pencil. Wind
the pencil round and round. Hang
up the mobile by the string.

Delta-Wing Jet

You will need

an expanded polystyrene ceiling tile, 30 cm square
glue for sticking material, such as Copydex
a small lump of plasticine
a strip of cardboard, about 10 cm long and 5 cm wide
3 long, big-headed pins
a big sheet of paper
a strong rubber band
a long cardboard box
a ruler and a ball-point pen
scissors and paints

Launch your jet and see how far and how fast you can make it fly. Or make two jets and have indoor or outdoor races.

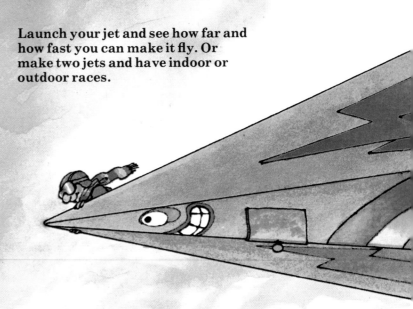

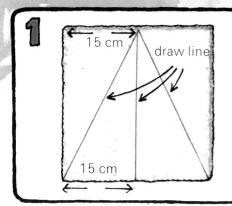

1 Measure 15 cm along the top and bottom of the tile and make marks. Draw a line between the two marks. Draw lines from the top mark to the two bottom corners (a).

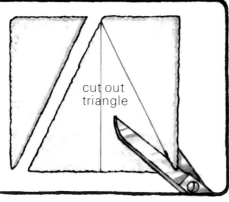

Carefully cut along the two lines from the top to the corners with scissors (b). Be careful not to break the cut-off pieces.

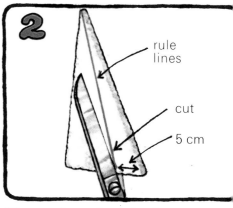

2 Measure 5 cm along the short edge of one cut-off piece. Draw a line from the mark to the point. Cut along the draw line. Throw away the small cut-off piece.

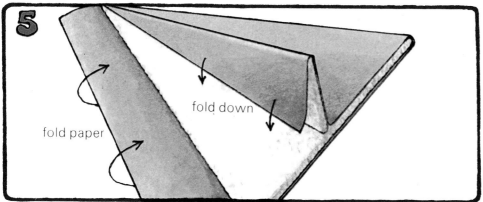

5 Put the jet down on a large sheet of paper. Fold the paper round the wings very neatly. Press it up the fin and glue the edges of the paper together.

Trim the edges of the paper on the fin. When the glue is dry, paint the paper in different colours.

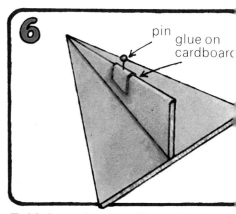

6 Fold the strip of cardboard in half. Glue it to the fin, about half-way along. Push a big-headed pin into the middle of the cardboard strip, like this.

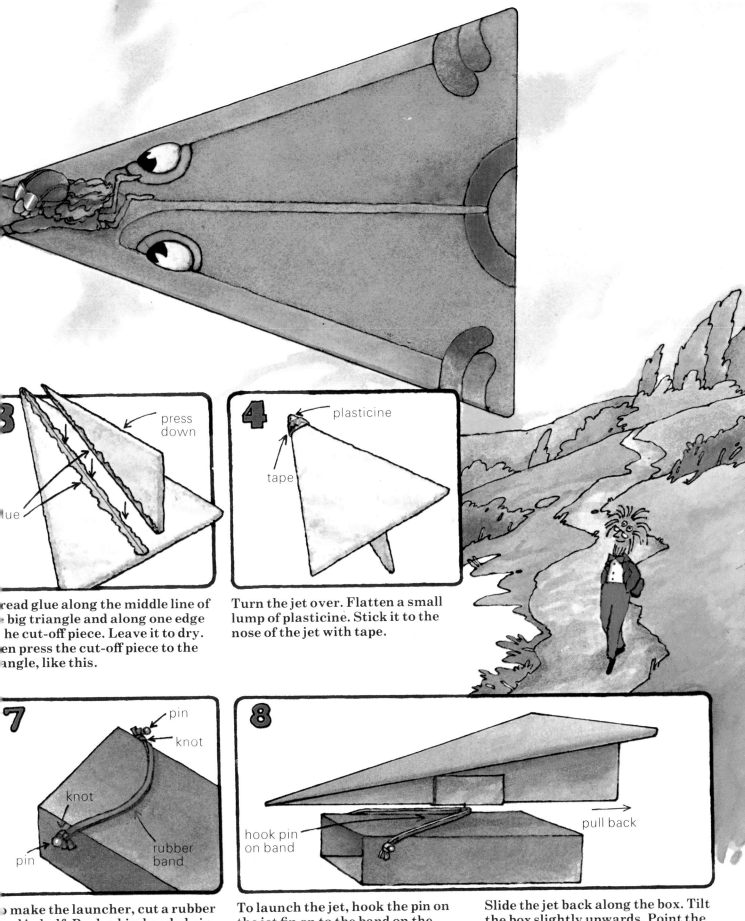

3

press down

glue

read glue along the middle line of
big triangle and along one edge
he cut-off piece. Leave it to dry.
en press the cut-off piece to the
angle, like this.

4

plasticine

tape

Turn the jet over. Flatten a small
lump of plasticine. Stick it to the
nose of the jet with tape.

7

pin

knot

knot

pin

rubber band

make the launcher, cut a rubber
nd in half. Push a big-headed pin
to each side of a long cardboard
x. Tie the ends of the band to the
g-headed pins.

8

hook pin on band

pull back

To launch the jet, hook the pin on
the jet fin on to the band on the
launcher. Hold the jet fin and pull it
gently backwards.

Slide the jet back along the box. Tilt
the box slightly upwards. Point the
jet and let it go.

Dandy, The Dashing Dragon

Pull up the curtain ring on the Dragon's head and let it go to make him rush along.

You will need
a piece of cardboard, about 12 cm long and 12 cm wide
a lump of modelling clay
a rubber band
a plastic drinking straw
a piece of nylon thread or very thin string, about 70 cm long
a small curtain ring
a big hairpin
a piece of thin paper, about 12 cm wide and 60 cm long
sticky tape and glue
scissors

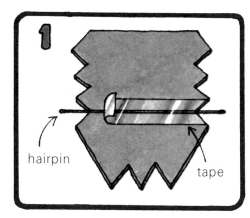

Cut a head shape out of cardboard, like this. Straighten a hairpin. Stick the pin with tape across the head, quite close to one end.

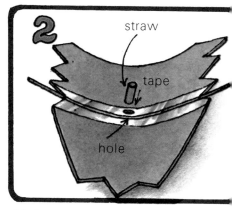

Make a hole in the middle of the head, just behind the hairpin. Pus a short piece of straw into the hole Glue it in place. Bend the head int curved shape.

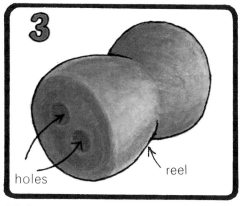

Make a reel, about 4 cm long and 3 cm across, out of modelling clay in this shape. Make two holes right through it, like this.

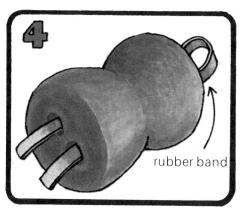

Cut a rubber band. Push the ends through the two holes in the clay reel, like this. Leave the reel until it is dry.

Knot the ends of the rubber band. Tie one end of the nylon thread on the reel. Wind all the thread on to the reel. Push the free end throug the straw.

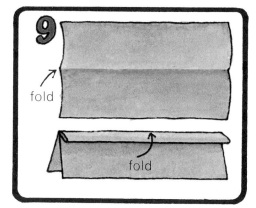

To make the dragon's body, fold the long piece of paper in half (a). Fold over the folded edge to make a flap about 1 cm wide (b).

Open out the paper. Make folds, about 2 cm wide, all along it, like this. Turn the paper over and crease all the folds the other way.

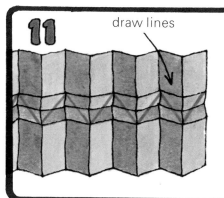

Open the paper again. Draw zig-za lines from the top fold line to the bottom fold line, like this.

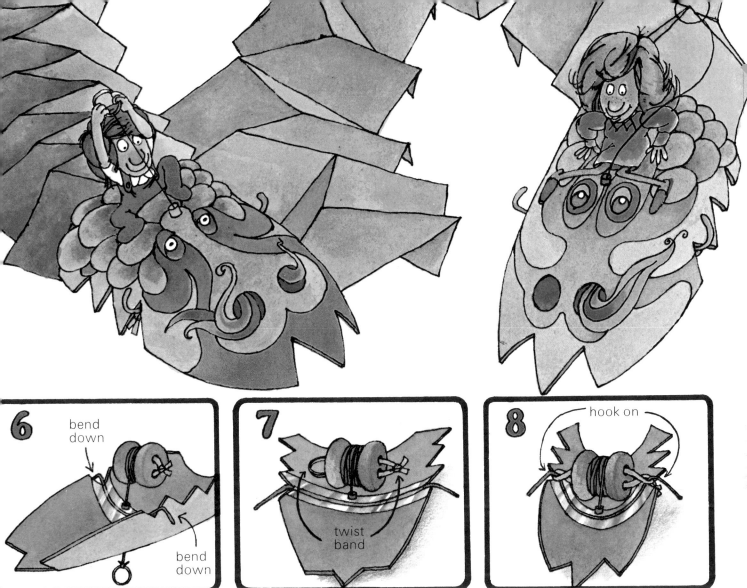

6

bend down

bend down

Tie one end of the thread to a curtain ring on top of the head. Bend the ends of the hairpin down.

7

twist band

Turn the reel round and round to wind the thread very tight. Give one twist to each end of the rubber band.

8

hook on

Hook each end of the rubber band on to the ends of the hairpin. Bend the head again to make sure the reel will not rub on it.

12

Fold the paper along all the drawn lines. Pinch together all the drawn lines and pleat the paper with your fingers, like this.

13

tape

Stick one end of the paper body to the edge of the cardboard head, like this. Paint the dragon's head with lots of different colours.

To make a longer tail, fold up a second strip of thin paper in the same way as the first one. Glue it to the end of the first strip.

Making a Periscope

With a periscope, you can see over the top of walls or over a crowd of people. You can make it as tall as you like if you have lots of cardboard.

You will need
a sheet of cardboard, about
    42 cm long and 42 cm wide
2 strips of cardboard about
    32 cm long and 8 cm wide
2 small mirrors, about 8 cm
    long and 6 cm wide
a pencil and a ruler
sticky tape and scissors

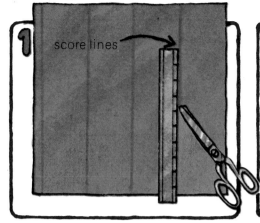

Measure four columns about 10 cm wide and one column 2 cm wide on the large sheet of cardboard. Put the ruler on each line and run the scissors along it to score it.

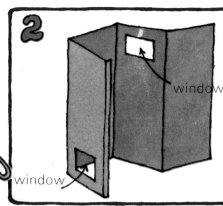

Fold the cardboard along the lines to make a long box. Cut a window, about 5 cm × 5 cm, near the bottom of one side and another near the top of the opposite side.

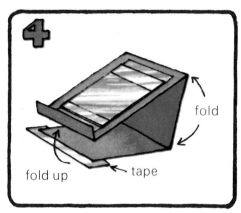

Measure three columns 8 cm wide and one column 2 cm wide on the two cardboard strips. Score along the lines. Stick a mirror on to each strip, like this.

Fold up the strips, with the mirrors on the outside, to make triangles. Bend up the flap of each strip and stick the ends to the flaps with tape, like this.

Put one triangle into the bottom of the box with the flap outside, like this. Stick the triangle to the box with tape.

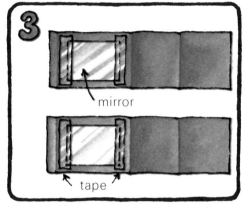

Turn the box upside down. Put in the second triangle so you can see the mirror through the window. Stick it in with tape. Close the box and stick the flap down.

Making a Kaleidoscope

old the kaleidoscope up to the
ht. Turn it slowly and watch
e patterns change.

ou will need
iece of cardboard, about
cm long and 24 cm wide
mall mirrors, each about
cm long and 6 cm wide
heet of greaseproof paper
iece of cellophane
all bits of coloured paper,
cellophane or drinking straws
encil and a ruler
cky tape and scissors

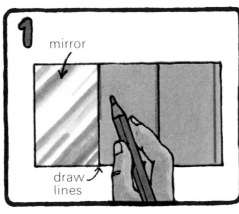

Put a mirror on the cardboard and
use it as a guide to draw three lines,
like this. Leave about 2 cm at one
end for a flap. Score the lines with
scissors.

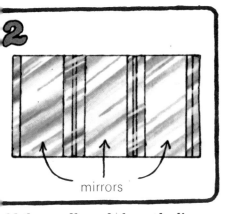

ld the cardboard along the lines.
ick the three mirrors to the
rdboard with tape, leaving little
aces between them, like this.

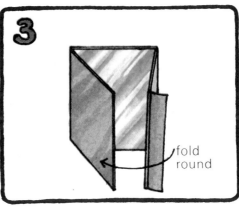

Fold the cardboard into a triangle
with the mirrors inside. Stick the
flap down with tape.

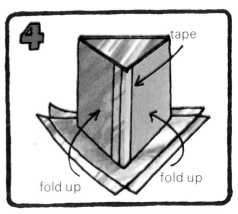

Cut two pieces of greaseproof paper
a little larger than the end of the
triangle. Stand the triangle on one
piece. Fold up the paper. Tape it to
the sides.

t the coloured paper, cellophane
drinking straws into very small
ts. Drop them into the top of the
iangle.

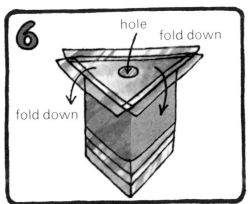

Cut a small hole in the second piece
of greaseproof paper. Put it over the
top of the triangle. Fold it down and
stick it to the sides with tape.

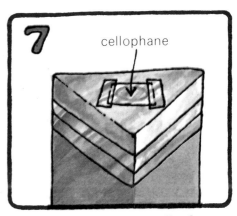

Stick the piece of clear cellophane
over the hole with tape. This is to
stop the coloured bits falling out.

Thank You Money Bank

Drop some money into the box and watch the sign come up. Turn the dials to keep a count of how much money you have.

You will need

a tall, thin box or a small cereal packet
a matchbox
3 used matchsticks
a sheet of thin cardboard
a piece of paper
a hairpin
2 small buttons
glue and sticky tape
scissors

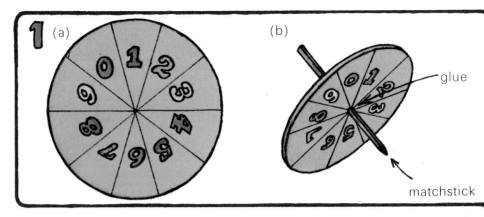

Cut three small circles out of thin cardboard. Draw five lines across each one. Write the numbers 0 to 9 in the sections of each circle (a).

Make a hole in the middle of each circle where the lines cross. Push a matchstick halfway through each hole (b). Glue the matchsticks to the circles.

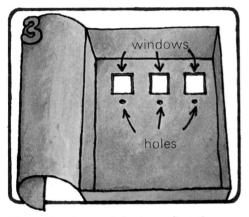

Open the door of the box. Cut three small windows in the front of the box, near the top. Make a hole underneath each window.

Push the matchsticks in the circles through the holes from inside the box. Look at the front of the box and make the windows a bit bigger if you cannot see the numbers.

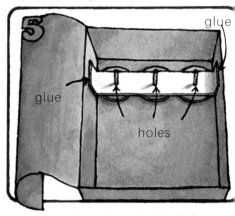

Cut a cardboard strip a little longer than the width of the box. Make three holes in it and push the matchsticks through. Glue the strip to the box sides.

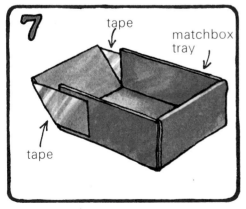

Cut down two corners of a matchbox tray. Bend down the end. Stick tape across the two corners, like this.

Cut a piece of paper a bit bigger than the matchbox tray. Write 'Thank You' on it. Glue it to a piece of cardboard the same size as the paper (a).

Glue one corner of the cardboard to a corner of the matchbox tray, like this. Make holes through the tray and cardboard. Straighten a hairpin and push it through (b).

2

stick
down
top

cut
round

...lue down the top of the box. Cut
...und three sides of the box, like
...is, to make a door.

6

push
in

hole

...old a matchbox cover against one
...de of the box. Draw round it. Cut
...long the lines. Push the cover
...alfway through the hole. Tip it
...own and glue it to the box.

9

hole

buttons

...ush a button on each end of the
...airpin. Make a hole in the box.
...ush the hairpin through, making
...ure the tray is just below the
...atchbox cover, like this.

10

draw
round

Hold the matchbox tray down and
draw a line round the 'Thank You'
sign on the inside of the box. Cut out
a window inside the lines.

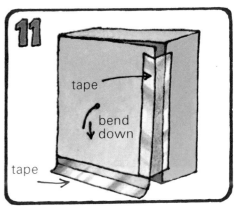

11

tape

bend
down

tape

Close the box door. Push the end of
the hairpin through it and bend it
down. Bend the hairpin down on the
front of the box. Stick the door all
the way round with tape.

Two-Stage Saturn Rocket

You will need

a long cardboard tube
2 short cardboard tubes
3 paper clips
2 rubber bands
a piece of string, about as long
    as the long tube
a piece of very thin cloth,
    about 20 cm long and 20 cm
    wide
4 pieces of cotton thread, each
    about 25 cm long
a small curtain ring
thick and thin cardboard
sticky tape and glue
scissors and a pencil

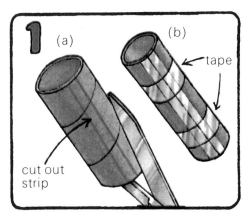

Slide a short cardboard tube into the long one. If it is too big, cut out a strip (a). Hold the cut edges together and stick them with tape to make a smaller tube (b).

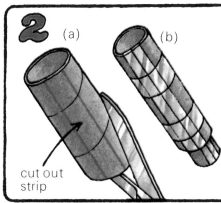

Cut a wider strip out of a second short tube (a). Stick the edges together with tape. Slide it inside the first tube (b).

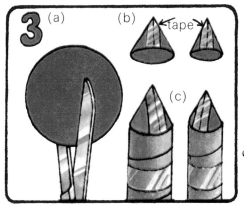

Cut a small circle out of thin cardboard. Cut it in half (a). Curl both halves into cones and stick with tape (b). Glue one cone to the top of each tube (c).

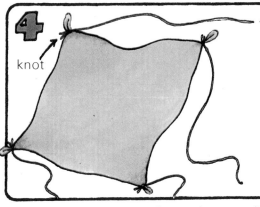

To make a drogue parachute, tie a piece of cotton thread tightly to each corner of the piece of cloth.

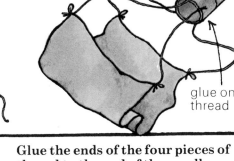

Glue the ends of the four pieces of thread to the end of the small rocket, like this. Make sure the threads are not twisted together.

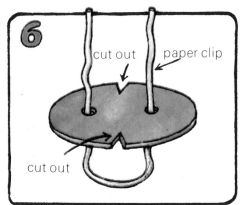

Cut two little triangles out of the edge of the cardboard circle. Straighten a paper clip. Push the ends through the holes in the circle, like this.

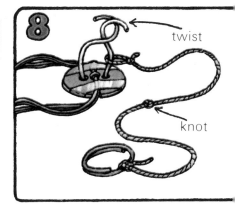

Loop two rubber bands together (a). Put them on the circle over the cut-out triangles (b). Stick them down with tape. Hook a paper clip on to the end of each band.

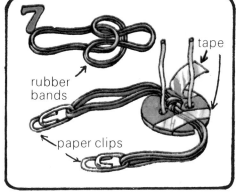

Twist the ends of the paper clip together and bend back. Tie the string on to the paper clip. Make a knot in the middle. Tie the curtain ring on the other end.

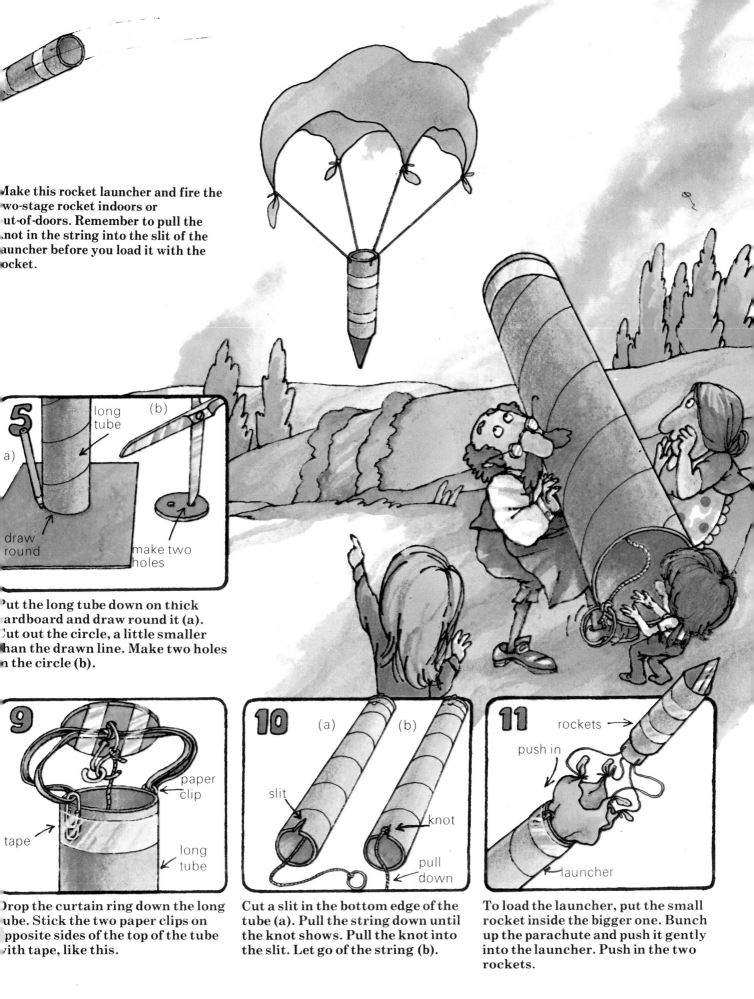

Make this rocket launcher and fire the two-stage rocket indoors or out-of-doors. Remember to pull the knot in the string into the slit of the launcher before you load it with the rocket.

5

(a)

(b)

long tube

draw round

make two holes

Put the long tube down on thick cardboard and draw round it (a). Cut out the circle, a little smaller than the drawn line. Make two holes in the circle (b).

9

paper clip

tape

long tube

Drop the curtain ring down the long tube. Stick the two paper clips on opposite sides of the top of the tube with tape, like this.

10

(a)

(b)

slit

knot

pull down

Cut a slit in the bottom edge of the tube (a). Pull the string down until the knot shows. Pull the knot into the slit. Let go of the string (b).

11

rockets

push in

launcher

To load the launcher, put the small rocket inside the bigger one. Bunch up the parachute and push it gently into the launcher. Push in the two rockets.

23

High-Wire Walker

Tie a very long piece of string across a room. Put the Walker on it. Push the plasticine to make it swing and move the Walker.

You will need
a matchbox
4 plastic drinking straws
a sheet of paper
a piece of thin cardboard
a piece of string, about 60 cm
    long
a long big-headed pin
plasticine
sticky tape and glue
scissors

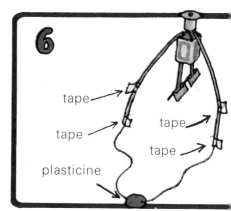

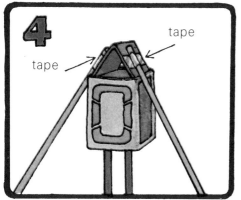

Cut a straw in half and then in half again. Push the tray half out of the matchbox. Stick two pieces of straw to the tray with tape to make legs. Push in the tray.

Cut two little slits in the end of each leg. Bend back the ends. Fold two small pieces of cardboard in half. Glue one to the end of each leg to make feet.

Cut a strip of cardboard about twi as long as the top of the matchbox. Fold it in half. Glue the ends to the top of the matchbox, like this.

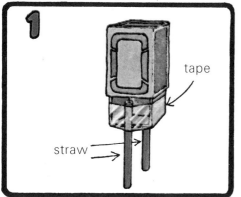

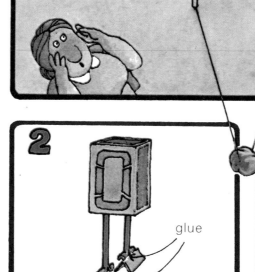

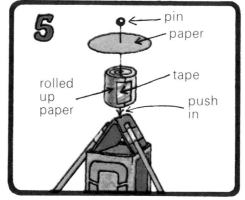

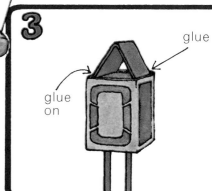

Stick a straw on each side of the folded cardboard with tape, like this, to make arms.

Roll up a thin strip of paper to make a head. Stick it with tape. Cut out a paper circle. Push the pin through it and into the head. Pin it to the top of the body.

Cut a straw in half. Stick one half each arm with tape. Stick the ends of the string on to the straws with tape. Put a lump of plasticine in th middle of the string.

Trick Cyclist

Balance the Cyclist on a very long piece of string. Tilt the string downwards to make the wheel roll round.

You will need
a piece of cardboard, about
    30 cm long and 15 cm wide
a cardboard tube
a drinking straw
a hairpin
a sheet of paper
plasticine
a pencil
glue and scissors

Draw a thin man, about 30 cm tall, on cardboard. Make the legs about twice as long as the body. Cut out the shape, with a wide space between the legs, like this.

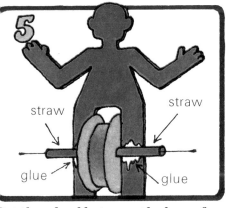

Put the end of a cardboard tube on some cardboard and draw two circles. Cut out the circles, about cm wider than the lines.

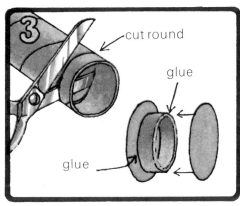

Cut a band, about 1 cm wide, off the end of the tube (a). Glue a circle on each side of the band to make a wheel (b).

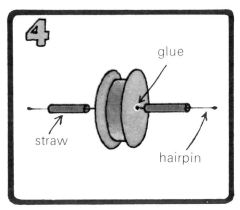

Straighten a hairpin and push it through the middle of the wheel. Glue it to the wheel. Push a short bit of straw on the hairpin on each side of the wheel.

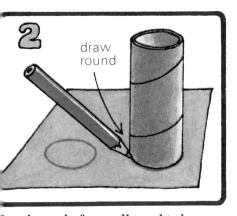

Put the wheel between the legs of he cardboard man, with a gap at he top. Make sure the wheel turns asily. Glue the two bits of straw to he legs, like this.

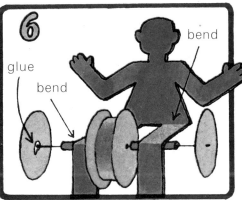

Bend the man's legs round the straw and bend him again at the top of his legs. Cut out two small paper circles. Glue one to each end of the hairpin.

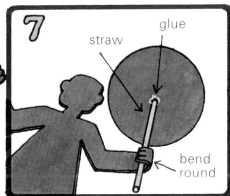

Cut out a paper circle. Glue it to the end of a bit of straw. Glue the other end to the man's hand. Glue a small lump of plasticine to the ends of the man's legs.

Fire-Fighting Truck

You will need
a shoe box, or an oblong
  cardboard box
a small cardboard box
4 empty cotton reels
very thin string
3 rubber bands
3 strips of thick cardboard, each
  about 30 cm long and 6 cm wide
2 paper fasteners
2 used matchsticks
3 pencils or thin sticks
a ball-point pen, without the
  ink tube, and a balloon
a plastic carton
scissors and glue

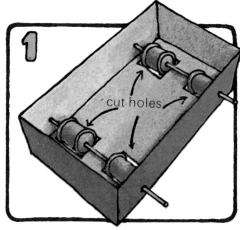

Cut four square holes in the shoe box bottom. Make two holes in each side. Push two pencils through one side. Slide two cotton reels on to each pencil and push out the sides.

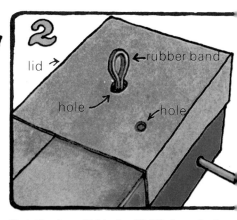

Cut the box lid in half. Make a hole in the middle of one half. Push a rubber band end through and slide on a matchstick underneath. Make a second hole. Put on the lid.

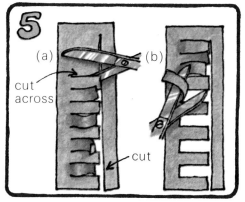

Cut up one side of the second cardboard strip. Then cut across (a). Cut out every other piece (b) to make a ladder. Cut a second ladder in the same way.

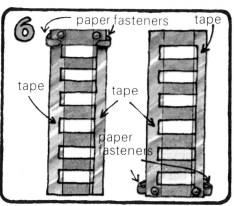

Put sticky tape down the sides of each ladder. Push two paper fasteners through the top of one ladder and the bottom of the other. Bend over the ends, like this.

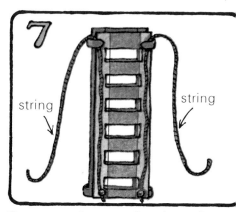

Cut two strings, each twice as long as the ladders. Put the two ladders together, like this. Tie a string to each bottom fastener and loop it over the top ones.

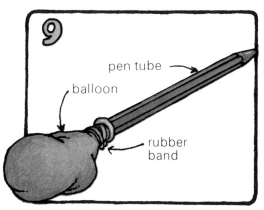

Push the pen tube into the neck of the balloon. Wind a rubber band round the balloon neck several times to make it very tight.

To fill the balloon, put the pen tube up a water tap. Turn on the tap. When the balloon is about as big as an orange, put the pen top on very quickly.

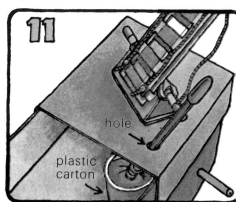

Put the balloon in a plastic carton to catch the drips of water. Push the pen tube through the hole in the box lid from the inside.

26

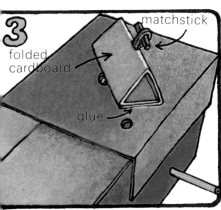

3

matchstick
folded cardboard
glue

...old a strip of cardboard up to make ...triangle, like this. Make a hole in ...e flat side and one fold. Push the ...nd through. Slide a matchstick ...rough loop of the band.

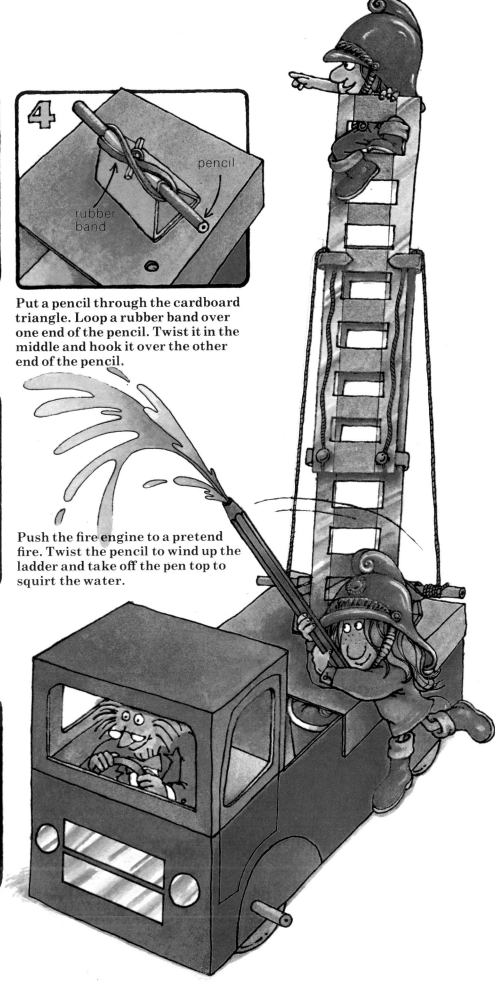

4

pencil
rubber band

Put a pencil through the cardboard triangle. Loop a rubber band over one end of the pencil. Twist it in the middle and hook it over the other end of the pencil.

Push the fire engine to a pretend fire. Twist the pencil to wind up the ladder and take off the pen top to squirt the water.

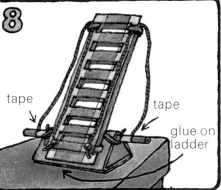

8

tape
tape
glue on ladder

...lue the underneath ladder to the ...riangle on the box lid. Wind the ...nd of each string round the pencil ...nd stick it with tape.

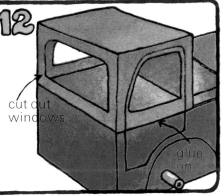

12

cut out windows
glue on

...o make a cab, cut out the sides of ...small box for the windscreen and ...de windows. Glue the box to the ...ont of the fire truck.

Moving Pictures

Caging a Rabbit

Twist up the string and then pull it tight to make the picture spin. Watch what happens.

You will need
a sheet of white cardboard
a piece of string, about 1 metre
    long
a pencil
paints or crayons
scissors

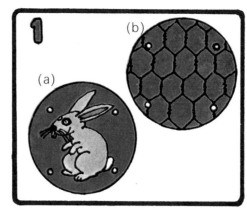

Cut out a circle of cardboard. Make four holes in it, near the edges. Draw and paint a rabbit on one side **(a)**. Draw a wire cage on the other side **(b)**.

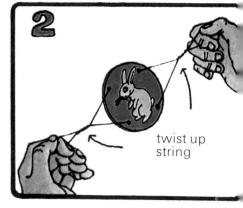

Thread one end of the string through the holes. Knot the ends together. Hold the two loops of the string, like this, and spin the circle round several times.

Pecking Duck

Pull and push the paper quickly up and down and watch the duck.

You will need
a piece of lined paper about
    12 cm long and 12 cm wide
a piece of plain paper about
    12 cm long and 8 cm wide
a piece of cardboard, about
    12 cm long and 8 cm wide
a pencil and a ruler
sticky tape and scissors
paints or crayons

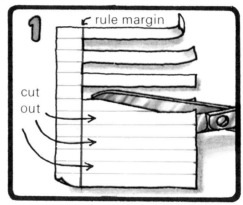

Rule a margin, about 2 cm wide, down one side of the lined paper. Cut along the lines to the margin. Cut out every other strip. Fold the strips along the margin.

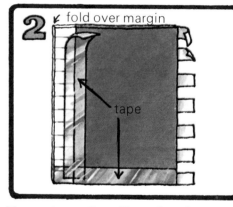

Put a piece of cardboard under the folded margin. Stick it down with tape. Stick a strip of tape along the bottom edge of the cardboard and fold it over.

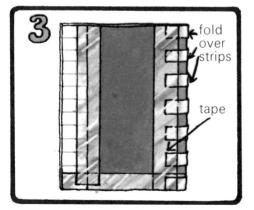

Fold all the ends of the strips round the cardboard. Stick them down with tape. Make sure they are even spaces apart.

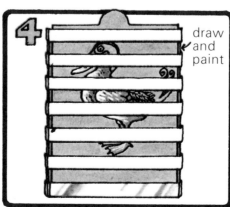

Slide the unlined paper between the cardboard and the strips. Draw and paint a duck on the paper in between the strips, like this.

When the paint is dry, pull the paper up so the duck disappears. Draw and paint a pecking duck and its food on the paper in the new spaces, like this.

trip Cartoon

ld the box up to the light.
ok through the eye hole and
n the bottom tube to watch
e film show.

u will need

nall cardboard box, about
5 cm long and 10 cm wide
rdboard tubes
iece of cardboard
eet of paper
ng strip of cellophane or
hort strips joined with tape
easeproof or see-through paper
-tipped pens
ky tape and glue
ssors

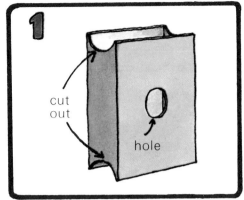

1

Cut the top and bottom off the box.
Cut a circle for an eye hole in one
side. Cut out half-circles in both
sides at the top and bottom of the
box, like this.

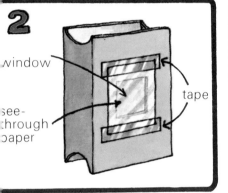

2

t a square window in the middle
the other side of the box. Stick a
uare of greaseproof paper over
e hole with tape.

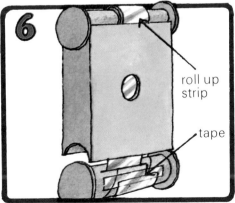

3

Draw four circles on cardboard,
using the end of a tube as a guide.
Cut out the circles a little larger
than the lines. Glue a circle on to
each end of the two tubes.

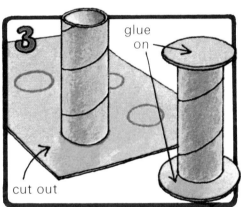

4

Cut a cellophane strip as wide as
the window in the box. Draw lines
on the strip to make boxes as high
as the window. Draw and colour a
story with a picture in each box.

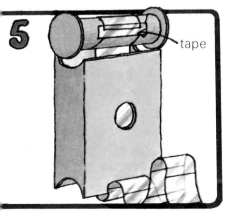

5

tick one end of the cellophane strip
one cardboard tube with tape.
ut the tube on the top of the box.
ush the strip through the box.

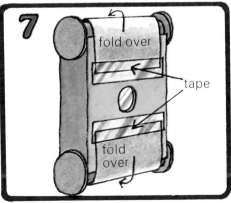

6

Cut a slit in both sides of the second
tube. Push the end of the strip
through. Stick it to the tube with
tape. Roll up the strip on to the top
tube.

7

Put a piece of paper over the top
tube and stick it to both sides of the
box with tape. Stick a second piece
over the bottom tube, like this.

Power Pacer

Wind the propeller on this boat about 20 times. Put the boat in water and let it go.

You will need
a plastic squeezy bottle
a piece of plastic cut from the side of a plastic bottle
a ball-point pen, with the ink tube taken out
3 strong rubber bands
a piece of thin bendy wire, about 10 cm long
a used matchstick
kitchen foil
scissors

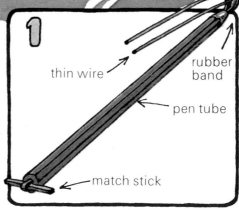

1 thin wire · rubber band · pen tube · match stick

Push a rubber band through the pen tube. Push a matchstick through the loop at one end. Hook a piece of bendy wire through the other end.

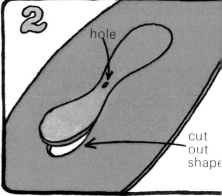

2 hole · cut out shape

To make the propeller, draw the shape of a figure eight, about 6 cm long, on the plastic piece. Cut it out. Make a small hole in the middle.

3 wind round · wind round

Push the ends of the wire through the hole in the propeller. Wind them tightly round, like this.

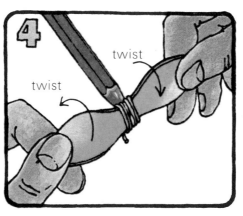

4 twist · twist

Hold the ends of the propeller like this. Twist the right side towards you and the left side away from you.

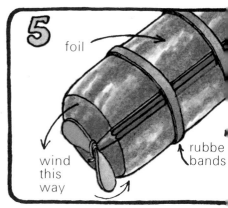

5 foil · wind this way · rubber bands

Wrap the plastic bottle tightly in foil. Put the pen tube against one side, with the propeller sticking out from the flat end. Put on two rubber bands, like this.

Balloon Record Breaker

Try making two boats and have races with them. The bigger you blow up the balloon, the faster and farther the boat will go.

You will need
- plastic squeezy bottle
- ball-point pen, with the ink tube taken out
- balloon
- small rubber band
- plasticine
- scissors

1

Push one blade of the scissors into one side of the plastic bottle. Cut out a long, wide strip, like this.

2

rubber band
balloon
pen tube

Push the pen tube into the neck of the balloon. Wind a rubber band very tightly round the neck of the balloon.

3

hole

Make a hole in the plastic bottle on the opposite side to the cut-out side. Push the balloon through the hole from the outside.

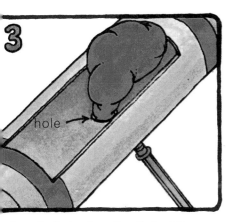

4

rubber band
plasticine

Bend back the pen tube towards the flat end of the bottle. Put a rubber band round it, like this, to keep it in place. Press some plasticine round the pen tube.

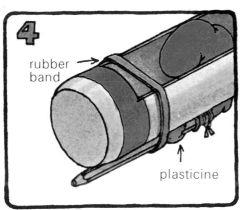

5

blow in here

To make the boat go along, blow up the balloon through the pen tube. Put the boat quickly in water and let it go.

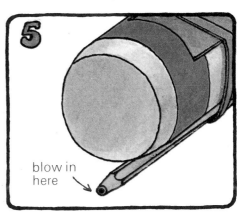

Hook-Up Tower Crane

You will need
a thin box, about 40 cm long
2 sticks, each about 60 cm long
2 short sticks
2 pencils
2 matchbox covers
a cardboard box
3 pieces of string, each about
    1½ metres long
2 big nails
2 strips of thick cardboard
a plastic carton
a tall, glass jar
plasticine
glue and sticky tape
scissors

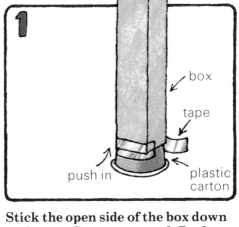

1 Stick the open side of the box down with tape. Cut out one end. Push a plastic carton, bottom end first, into the box end. Stick it in place with tape, like this.

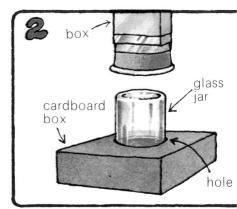

2 Cut a round hole in the square box. Push in a tall, glass jar. Sit the carton in the tall box on the jar. This is the base of the crane and should turn round easily.

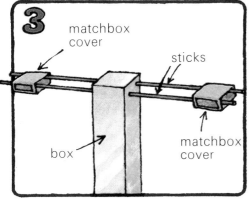

3 Slide a matchbox cover on to two long sticks. Make holes and push them through the top of the tall box, like this. Slide a second cover on to the other ends.

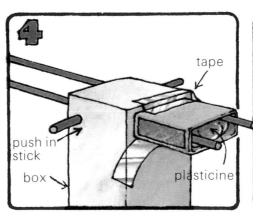

4 Tape one matchbox cover very firmly to the tall box. Push lots of plasticine into it. Make holes in the top of the tall box and push a short stick through.

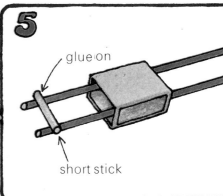

5 Glue a short piece of stick across the ends of the two long sticks, like this. Make sure the matchbox cover slides easily along the long sticks.

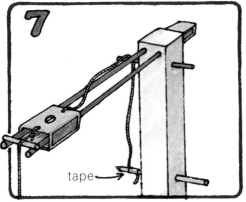

7 Push a pencil through the tall box, about half-way up. Slide the cover to the end of the sticks. Loop one string over the short stick and tape the end to the pencil.

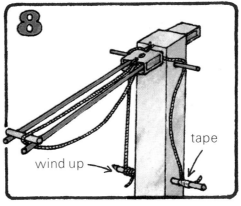

8 Wind the pencil to slide the cover along to the box. Loop the second string over the stick ends, through the cover and over the short stick. Tape the end to the pencil.

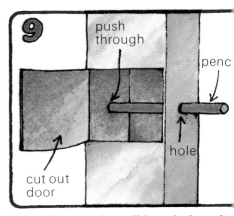

9 Cut a door in the tall box, below the pencil. Push a second pencil through one side of the box and out the other side, like this.

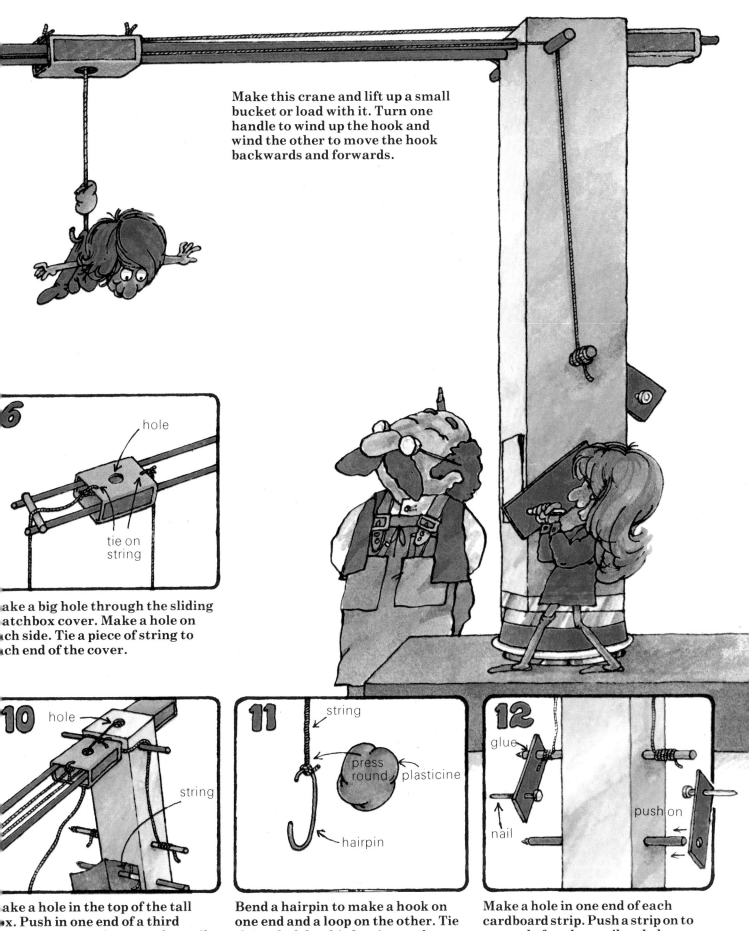

Make this crane and lift up a small bucket or load with it. Turn one handle to wind up the hook and wind the other to move the hook backwards and forwards.

6

hole

tie on string

ake a big hole through the sliding atchbox cover. Make a hole on ch side. Tie a piece of string to ch end of the cover.

10

hole

string

ake a hole in the top of the tall x. Push in one end of a third ring. Tape it to the second pencil. t the other end through the hole the sliding cover.

11

string

press round plasticine

hairpin

Bend a hairpin to make a hook on one end and a loop on the other. Tie the end of the third string to the loop. Press plasticine round the loop and knot.

12

glue

nail

push on

Make a hole in one end of each cardboard strip. Push a strip on to one end of each pencil and glue them on. Push a nail through the other end of each strip.

Eager Weaver

Wind the two tubes round to move the woven part along the box. Use different coloured wools on the shuttle to make woven patterns. C tie different colours to the tubes.

Make this loom and use it to weave small scarves, ties and belts. Or weave long pieces and sew them together to make patchwork blankets.

You will need
a cardboard shoe box or strong
    cardboard box
thick cardboard
2 long cardboard tubes
4 large rubber bands
coloured wools
a pencil and a ruler
glue and sticky tape
scissors

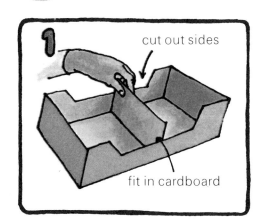

Cut out the sides of the box, like this. Cut a piece of cardboard for the handle, about 9 cm wide and as long as the width of the box. Make sure it fits the box.

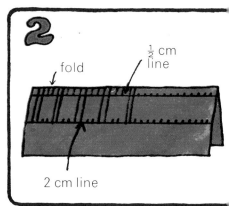

Fold the cardboard in half. Rule lines $\frac{1}{2}$ cm and 2 cm from the fold. Mark every $\frac{1}{2}$ cm along both lines. Rule long and short boxes, with a space between them, like this.

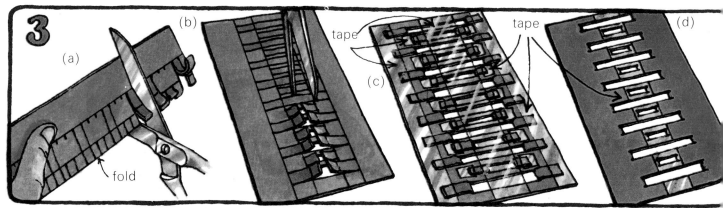

Cut along all the lines from the fold (a). Unfold the cardboard. Snip every other cut bit along the fold (b).

When all the bits have been cut, fold them back. Fold the short cuts back to the $\frac{1}{2}$ cm line and the long cuts to the 2 cm line. Stick all the flaps down with tape (c).

Stick tape along the fold on both sides of the cardboard (d). Snip out all the bits of tape in the spaces. Th piece of cardboard is the heddle.

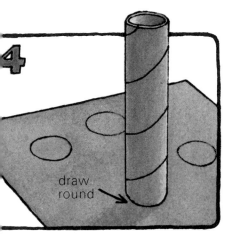

4

Using the end of a tube as a guide, draw four circles on cardboard. Cut out the circles a little larger than the lines. Glue a circle to each end of the tubes.

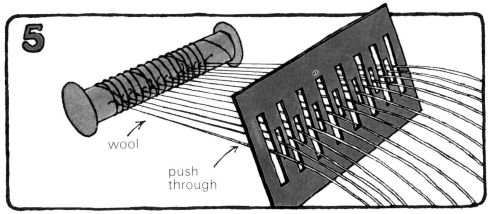

5

Cut 15 pieces of wool at least 50 cm long. Knot one piece round one end of a tube. Push the other end through the first hole in the heddle.

Tie on another piece of wool. Push it through the second hole in the heddle. Tie on the rest of the wool, pushing it through the holes in the heddle, like this.

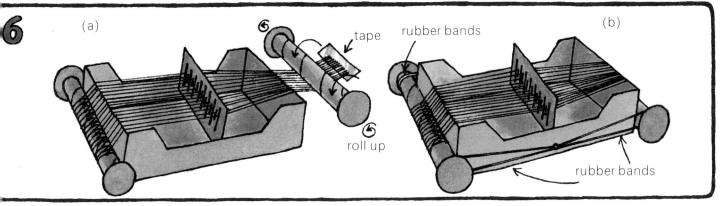

6

(a)

(b)

tape

rubber bands

roll up

rubber bands

Put the heddle in the middle of the box. Put the tube with the wool on the outside at one end. Pull all the free ends of the wool over the other end of the box.

Put a second tube over the ends of the wool. Stick the ends to the tube with tape (a).

Knot two rubber bands together. Hook them over the tubes on one side of the box (b). Knot two more bands and hook them on to the other ends of the tubes.

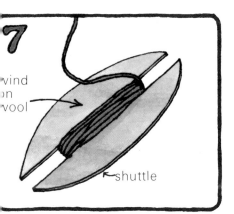

7

wind on wool

shuttle

Cut out a piece of cardboard a little longer than the width of the box. Cut into this shape. This is the shuttle. Wind on a very long piece of wool, like this.

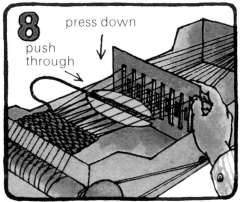

8

press down

push through

Tie the end of the wool on the shuttle to a strand of wool on the loom. Press the heddle down and push the shuttle through between the strands of wool.

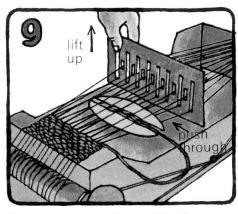

9

lift up

push through

To weave the next line, lift the heddle up. Push the shuttle through from the other side. Push the heddle against the woven part each time you weave a new line.

35

Sailing Yacht

You will need

1 expanded polystyrene ceiling
   tile, 30 cm square
a thin stick, about 40 cm long
a ball-point pen
a strong plastic bag
2 empty toothpaste tubes
15 paper fasteners
strong thread or thin string
a long, big-headed pin
a hairpin and a rubber band
a needle and thread
kitchen foil and small nails
scissors

1

draw shape
cut out

Draw the shape of a boat, about
25 cm long, on the tile. Cut it out
with scissors. Wrap the boat
tightly in foil, smoothing down the
sides and edges.

When you sail your boat, look at the
flag to see which way the wind is
blowing. If it is this way, let both
sails out as far as they will go and
put the hairpin straight.

WIND

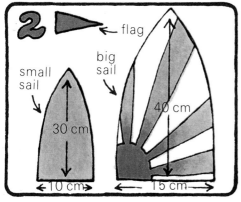

2 flag

small sail
big sail
30 cm
40 cm
10 cm
15 cm

Cut two sails out of a plastic bag in
these shapes. Make the big sail
about 40 cm high and the small one
about 30 cm high. Cut out a long thin
flag like this.

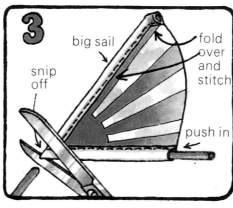

3

big sail
fold over and stitch
snip off
push in

Fold over one curved side and the
straight side of the big sail. Stitch
down the folds. Cut the corner off
the folded edges. Push in the stick
and pen, like this.

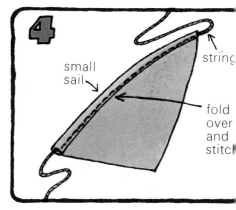

4

small sail
string
fold over and stitch

Cut a piece of string about 60 cm
long. Lay the string down along one
curved edge of the small sail. Fold
it over and stitch down the fold
round the string, like this.

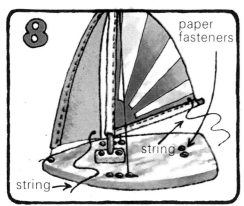

8

paper fasteners
string
string

Cut small holes in the corner of the
sails, like this. Tie a string to each
sail. Push in two paper fasteners on
each side of the boat and two at the
back of the boat.

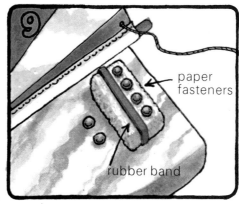

9

paper fasteners
rubber band

Cut a bit of tile about 5 cm long and
3 cm wide. Put a rubber band round
it. Push in four fasteners through
the bit and through the boat at the
back, like this.

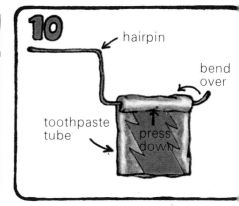

10

hairpin
bend over
toothpaste tube
press down

Cut the top and bottom off a
toothpaste tube. Bend a hairpin into
this shape. Fold one edge of the
tube over the hairpin to make a
rudder.

the wind is blowing from the left ...de, let the sails about half-way out ...d put the hairpin over to the left.

If the wind is blowing from the right side, let out the sails about half way. Put the hairpin over to the right.

If the wind is blowing towards you, your boat will blow back when you push it out. Go round the pond a little until the wind is on one side.

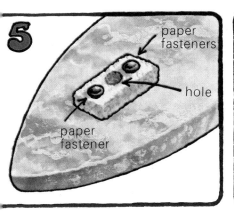

...ut out a bit of tile, about 6 cm long ...nd 3 cm wide. Make a hole in the ...iddle. Push a paper fastener into ...ch end and then through the boat, ...bout 6 cm from the front.

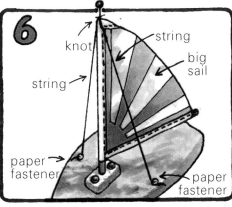

Put the stick in the hole, like this. Push a pin in the top. Tie on two pieces of string. Push in a paper fastener on each side of the stick. Tie on the strings.

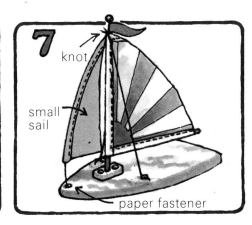

Tie one end of the small sail string to the pin. Push a paper fastener into the boat front and tie on the string. Fold the end of the flag round the pin and stitch it on.

...ush the end of the hairpin up ...rough the boat at the back, like ...is. Put the rubber band over the ...d of the hairpin.

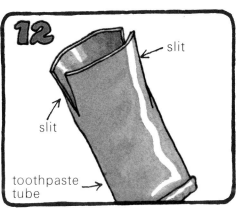

Cut the top off another toothpaste tube. Cut a slit down each side. Push in some nails and press the tube flat. This is for the keel which stops the boat blowing over.

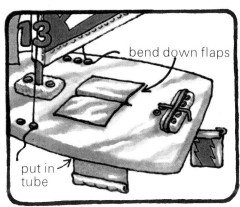

Make a slit in the middle of the boat, between the back and the mast. Push the tube through from underneath. Fold back the two flaps on top of the boat.

Mr Twitch

Turn Mr Twitch upside down to make his arms go round. When they stop, turn him up again.

You will need
2 plastic cartons or yoghurt pots
a piece of thin cardboard
4 used matchsticks
2 long needles
table salt
a drinking straw
glue and sticky tape
a needle and thread
a pencil and scissors

Draw four circles on thick cardboard, using the top of a plastic carton as a guide. Cut out the circles.

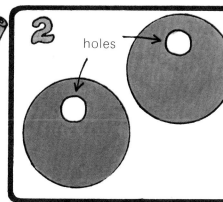

Cut a round hole in each of the cardboard circles, near one edge, like this.

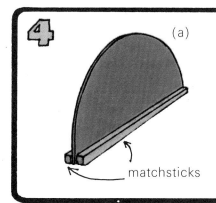

Fold a third cardboard circle in half. Cut along the fold. Glue a matchstick on each side of one half-circle (a). Glue matchsticks to the other half-circle.

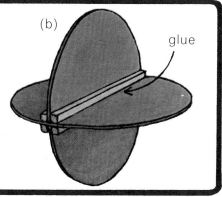

Glue the uncut circle to the matchsticks on one half-circle. Glue the second half-circle to the circle, like this (b).

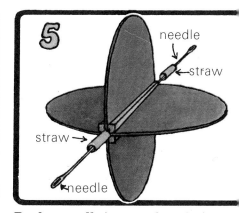

Push a needle into each end of the matchsticks. Slide a very short bit of straw on to the end of each needle.

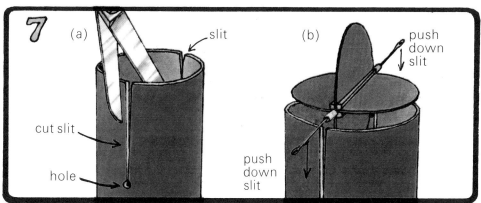

Stand the tube on end and cut two slits about half-way down it on both sides (a). Make a small hole at the end of each slit.

Push the cardboard circles down inside the tube with the needles in the slits (b). Spin the circles to make sure they turn easily. If not, trim a bit off the circles.

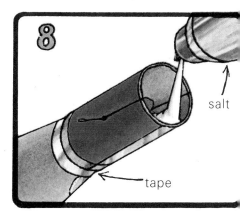

Pour some table salt into the tube. Put in enough to almost fill the plastic carton.

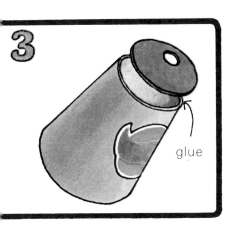

3

lue one cardboard circle to the
p of each of the plastic cartons.
se lots of glue to stick them very
mly.

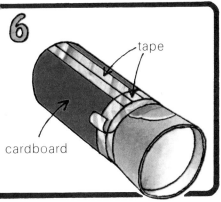

6

tape

cardboard

oll a piece of thin cardboard very
ghtly round the top of a plastic
rton. Stick it with tape to make a
be. Tape the tube very firmly to the
rton.

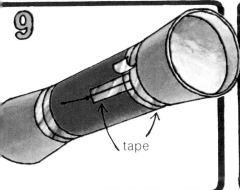

9

tape

ush the top of the second plastic
rton into the top of the tube.
rap sticky tape very tightly round
e end of the tube to stick it to the
rton.

10

thread

knot

Cut the shape of two long arms out
of thin paper. Cut them at the
elbows. Cut out fingers and thumbs.
Use a needle and thread to join
the arms and fingers, like this.

11

glue

glue

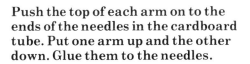

Push the top of each arm on to the
ends of the needles in the cardboard
tube. Put one arm up and the other
down. Glue them to the needles.

Formula XF Bullet

You will need

a sheet of paper, 29 cm long
and 21 cm wide
2 ball-point pens without
the ink tubes
a ball-point pen top
2 plastic drinking straws or
very thin sticks
a bead
bendy wire and a paper clip
a matchbox cover
thick cardboard
stiff plastic cut from a
plastic bottle
a strong rubber band
glue and sticky tape
a pencil and scissors

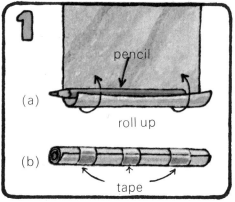

Put the pencil on one edge of the paper. Roll the paper very tightly round the pencil (a). Stick the end of the rolled paper with tape (b). Shake out the pencil.

Cut two small circles out of cardboard, for the front wheels. Use a cotton reel as a guide. Cut out two big circles for the back wheels. Use a cup as a guide.

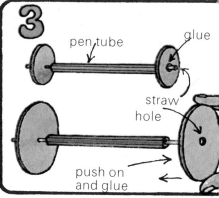

Make a hole in the middle of each wheel. Push a straw through a pen tube. Push a small wheel on each end and glue them on. Do the same with the back wheels.

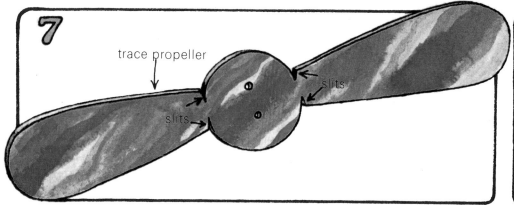

Trace this propeller shape on thin or see-through paper. Cut out the shape. Hold it down on a piece of plastic. Draw round the shape.

Cut the shape out very carefully. Cut two little slits on each side of the round part. Make two holes in the round middle part.

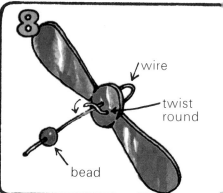

Loop a piece of bendy wire through the holes in the propeller. Twist one end round the other end, like this. Push the long end through a bead and pull it tight.

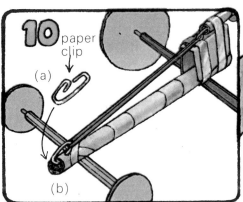

4 tape, tape, tape, paper tube

t the paper tube across the two
n tubes, like this. Wind sticky
pe round the paper tube and each
n tube to fix them in place.

5 matchbox cover, tape, tape, big wheel

Cut one side off a matchbox cover.
Put it, cut side down, on the paper
tube at the end with the big wheels.
Tilt it forward a little, like this,
and stick it to the tube with tape.

6 cut off tip, tape

Cut the end of a pen top with
scissors. Put it on top of the
matchbox cover, like this. Stick
it down very firmly with tape.

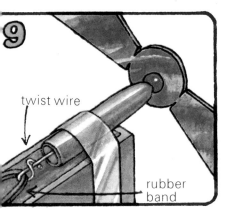

9 twist wire, rubber band

sh the long end of the wire
rough the pen top on the car.
op a rubber band on to the wire
d twist the wire round, like this.

10 paper clip (a) (b)

Bend open a paper clip (a). Push one
loop into the end of the paper tube.
Hook the end of the rubber band
on to the other loop of the paper
clip (b).

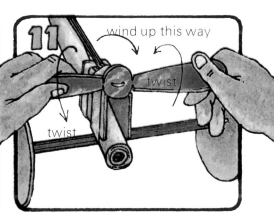

11 wind up this way, twist, twist

Hold the propeller like this. Twist
the right side towards the front of
the car. Twist the left side the other
way. Wind up the propeller this way
about 20 times.

Water Clock

Make this water clock and use it to tell the time. If the hand goes round too fast, drop a drawing pin or big-headed pin into the bottom of the plastic bottle. Or push a thin piece of stick into the hole. If the cork does not go down with the water, put a bit more plasticine on the string. Remember to empty the pot or bowl in the bottom of the box when it is full of water.

You will need

a plastic squeezy bottle
a large, strong cardboard box,
   about 40 cm high
2 knitting needles
2 corks
4 pieces of string, each about
   as long as the width of the box
a sheet of paper
a piece of cardboard
plasticine
a pot or bowl
a pencil
scissors and glue

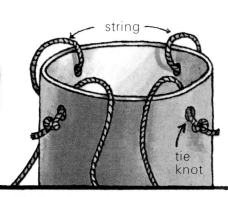

Cut the bottom off a plastic bottle. Make four holes in it, near the bottom edge (a).

Push a piece of string through each hole. Tie a knot on the end of each string on the outside of the bottle (b).

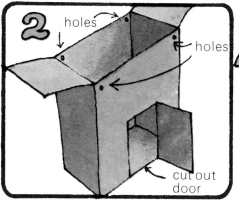

Open the top of the box. Cut a door in one side, near the bottom. Make a hole in each corner near the top of the box.

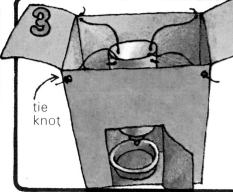

Put the bottle inside the box. Push one string through each hole in the top of the box and tie a knot on the end. Put a pot or bowl in the bottom of the box.

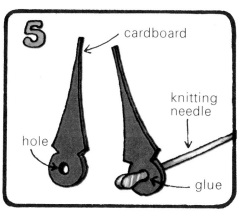

Cut out a paper circle. Write on it the numbers 1 to 12, like the face of a clock. Stick it to the front of the box, near the top. Make a hole in the middle of the circle.

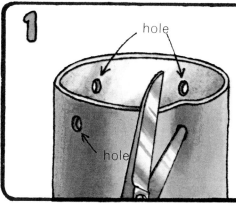

Cut a clock hand from a piece of cardboard. Make a hole in the round end (a). Push a knitting needle through the hole and glue the hand to the end (b).

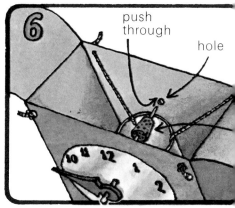

Make a hole through a cork with scissors. Push the knitting needle through the clock face. Push the cork on to the needle and push the needle out the back of the box.

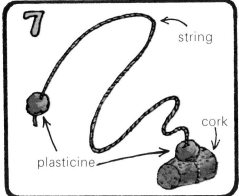

Cut a string a little longer than the height of the box. Tie a cork on one end. Put some plasticine on the string near the cork. Put another lump on the other end.

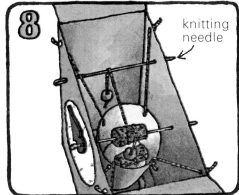

Put the string round the cork, like this. Drop the cork end into the bottle. Push a second knitting needle through the box near the first one. Loop the string over it.

Pour some water into the plastic bottle. Pull up the plasticine end of the string so that the cork just rests on the water.

Gallery Shoot Out

You will need

a large, oblong cardboard box
    with a lid
a small cardboard box
a sheet of thick cardboard
2 cotton reels
a long rubber band
a garden cane or thin stick
a pencil
8 drawing pins
a ball-point pen with the ink
    tube taken out
short pieces of drinking straw
2 long, big-headed pins
scissors, sticky tape and glue

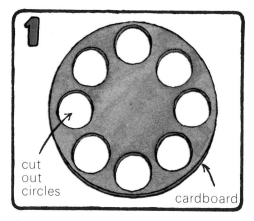

Cut out a circle of cardboard, small
enough to fit inside the bottom
of the large box. Cut out eight
small circles, like this.

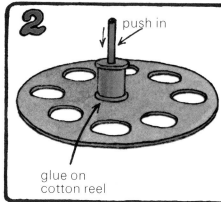

Make a hole in the middle of the
circle. Glue a cotton reel over the
hole. Push a pencil through the
cotton reel and then the hole.

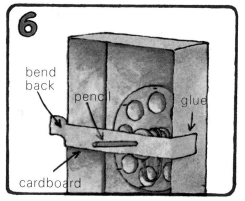

Cut a cardboard strip a little longer
than the box width. Make a hole in
the middle. Push the pencil through
the hole. Bend over the ends and
glue them to the box.

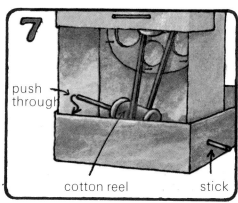

Make a hole in each side of the box.
Push a stick through one side. Glue
a reel to the middle of the stick.
Loop the band round it. Push the
stick out the other side.

Cut out eight small circles of
cardboard. Make a hole in each one
near the edge. Draw faces on them
and hook them on the drawing pins
on the large circle.

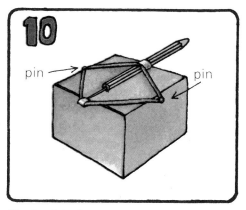

Push a big-headed pin into each
side of the small box. Put the pen
tube on top of the box. Hook the
rubber band round the pins.

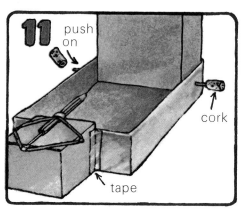

Stick the small box to the end of
the big box with tape, like this.
Make a hole in two corks. Push
them on to each end of the stick.

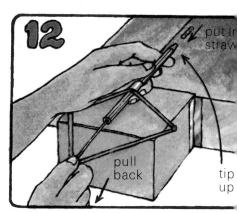

To fire the gun, hold the pen tube
and tip the end upwards. Drop a
bit of straw down the end. Pull back
the ink tube, aim at a face in the box
and let go the end.

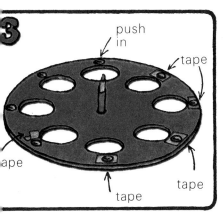

3

push
in

tape

tape

ape

tape

rn the circle over. Push drawing
...s through it, just above each of
... eight holes. Stick a bit of tape
...er each one.

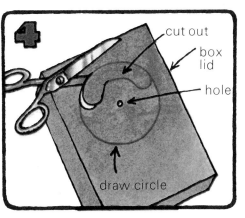

4

cut out

box
lid

hole

draw circle

Make a hole in the middle of the lid
of the large box. Put the circle down
on the lid and draw round it. Cut out
a shape in the lid, like this.

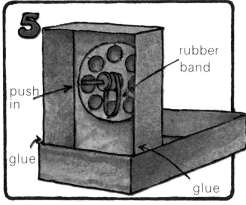

5

rubber
band

push
in

glue

glue

Stand the box bottom in the lid, like
this. Glue it at the sides and end.
Push the pencil in the circle through
the hole in the lid. Put a rubber band
on the reel.

9

pen
tube

rubber
band

tape

tape

...ke the ink tube out of a pen. Push
... wrong end into the pen. Loop a
...bber band round the pen, like
...s, and stick it with tape. Stick the
...nd to the ink tube.

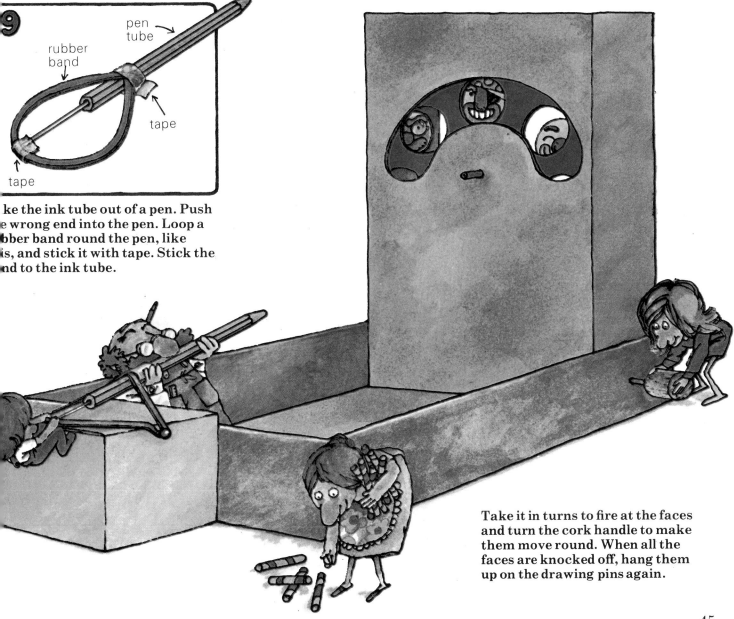

Take it in turns to fire at the faces
and turn the cork handle to make
them move round. When all the
faces are knocked off, hang them
up on the drawing pins again.

Grand Prix Car Races

Make this track and race your toy cars all round the floor. It will work best on a floor without a carpet. You can make the circuits any shape you like by putting the strings round more chair legs. If the strings slip on the wheels, push the chairs away from the wheels to make them tight again.

Before a race, decide how many times the cars should go round the tracks. It could be twice for a short race or ten times for a long one. The winner is the first car to reach the finishing line.

You will need
2 small, toy cars
a round, cardboard cheese box
2 pieces of thick string, each
    about 5 metres long
2 horseshoe magnets
a sheet of sandpaper
2 big nails
2 pencils
2 ball-point pen tops
cardboard
4 empty tins
strong glue

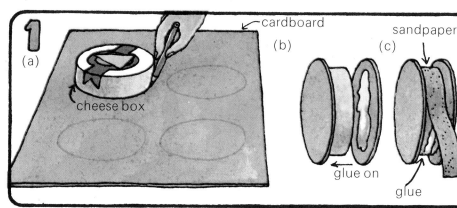

Draw four circles on cardboard, using the cheese box as a guide (a). Cut out the four circles, making them about 1 cm bigger than the drawn lines.

Glue two circles on each side of the cheese box lid and bottom to make two wheels (b). Glue a strip of sandpaper round the wheels (c).

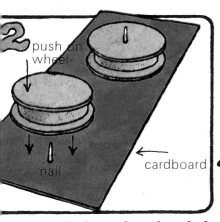

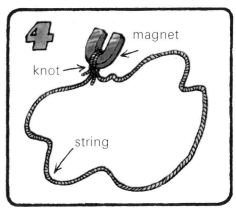

2 push on wheel

nail

cardboard

sh two nails through each end of rge sheet of cardboard. Stick iece of tape over each nail head. sh a nail through the middle of ch wheel, like this.

3 glue

pencil

glue

Glue a ball-point pen top over each nail. Make sure no glue goes on the nails. Push a pencil through each wheel near the edge. Glue them in place.

4 magnet

knot

string

Tie the ends of each piece of string together. Tie a magnet to the knot in each piece of string.

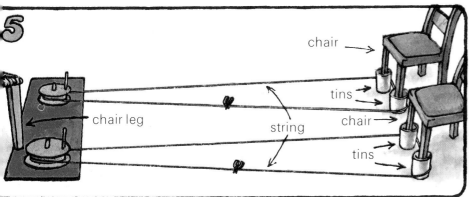

5 chair

tins

chair leg

string

chair

tins

t the cardboard with the wheels wn on the floor. Put a table or air leg on it. Loop one string und each wheel. Put the front s of two chairs in tins.

Put two chair legs over each string, like this. Push the chairs gently away from the wheels until the strings are stretched tight.

6 iron screw

tape

Try sticking the cars to the magnets. If they will not stick, put a small, fat, iron screw or bit of iron on the front of each car. Stick it firmly in place with tape.

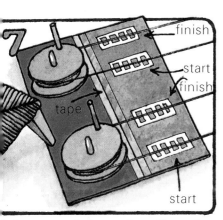

7 finish

start

finish

tape

start

8 wind this way

wind this way

ick a second piece of cardboard front of the first one with tape. aw or paint a starting and ishing line under each string.

To race the cars, wind the magnets back to the starting lines. Stick a car to each magnet. When someone says 'go', two players each wind a handle to move the cars forward.

If a car comes off a magnet, wind the handle the other way to move the magnet back again to the car. Or go to the car and stick it on the magnet again.